# Relief of My Symptoms

## Poems

## by Kevin Chesser

Ghost Palace Press
2023

First paperback edition 2023
Ghost Palace Press

*Book Design* by Jen Iskow
*Cover Design* by Bill Dunlap

ISBN 979-8-218-20015-2

Ghost Palace Press is an experimental art and publishing
studio based in Thomas, West Virginia

www.ghostpalacepress.com

*Yesterday? Was that real?*
-Perfect Blue

## Coffin

Yesterday, there was music everywhere. I heard it fending off a frog in the shithouse, then again when I pressed my ear against a knot in a tree. There were times when the music was bigger than the sky, and times when it was smaller than the tip of a mouse's tail. I hated this music. I hated yesterday, and am still shoveling dirt over its coffin.

## No Mercy

This story is about fireflies rotting in a jar. Just being aware of its existence will turn your life into a merciless environment.

The story starts with a baseball game, after school, on the cusp of summer break. Anthony Paranoia stole home. I wasn't there. I only heard about it later.

Later was when I was gathering fireflies for the jar. I gave them all names as I caught them, and the name was the same for each one - Our Lord Vlad.

Our Lord Vlad looked at Our Lord Vlad and told Our Lord Vlad to get Our Lord Vlad - something was up. They were being gathered for their beauty, a stupid reason. I asked Our Lord Vlad if they would talk to Our Lord Vlad and the others about the real meaning of beauty - that they themselves were not beautiful but that it was beautiful for me to be gathering them.

When they stopped glowing, their bodies rotted to goo. It didn't take very long.

People don't know about my hometown or the baseball game where Tony P. stole home. They don't know that I do beautiful things.

For these reasons, I have chosen to show no mercy.

I

# *Inheritance*

Alison and her two dogs were standing at the gate to a ranch in Texas. They had been walking all day. It was hot. The voice of dehydration said "a truck is coming this way." A truck was coming that way, from inside the ranch. The dogs saw some wild pigs and took off after them. Alison was relieved. The pigs would put the fear of God into them. Dogs need religion. She wished she had the time. The truck was getting closer. It was red. It slowed down for a roadrunner. The roadrunner paused and looked up at the sky. Alison looked up at the sky. Then the truck disappeared, like a ghost walking into a wall. She whistled for the dogs, and their new holy friends, the pigs.

## Comfort, Redefined

By the way, I've heard Texas is marvelous this time of year,
a little windy. Can you guess what else is on my mind lately?
It's the amount of space you're taking up in my house. You're
on my couch, my comfy couch. You're in the kitchen dancing
with the roaches. Showering until the dead rise from their
graves. You're on the patio, smoking cigars with my neighbor
Mussolini. Sprawled out on the dining room table, wearing
nothing but a tea cup. You left my handgun, loaded, on the
shelf in the garage next to the potting soil. I nearly planted
a gun tree! And those take forever to mature. Sort of like
you. At night we watch movies and talk. It seems we have
no choice. Have you seen this one before? It's about an FBI
agent who plants a garden. He's not depressed or dealing
with a crisis or anything. He does it for the vegetables. All
in all, he's a pretty decent agent, though he did get all those
people killed in Texas. Your flight leaves in the morning.

## *Ancient Grains*

Mom was there, way off in the distance. I was five years old, waist deep in the wild-at-heart suburban water. That water was air conditioned. I prayed a salamander back to life. This was dad's birthday. I knew what to give him. He loved that salamander. More than I ever could. With it resting in his hand dad became calm and ate so much bread. That house was air conditioned. But I kept thinking about going back out in the water. I'd have to wait until later, after dad and the salamander were asleep. This left no small amount of time to kill. I stood and looked at myself in the mirror for a while. The buttery grains of my eyes started to run out of my face and onto the floor. "Oh shit," I said, waking up dad and the salamander.

My punishment was to stand at the window until morning. Not so bad. Saw the moon come up. Saw mom out there, way off in the distance, digging a hole for the whole Earth.

## Over Creeks and Pastures

The twins were walking somewhere. They'd left the trail hours ago and the one named Jacques was starting to get annoyed. Jacques said to the other twin, whose name was Jan, "This little outing's gone on long enough, don't you agree?" But Jan did not agree. He wanted to find the hermit's cave, where there was treasure, or a stack of nudie magazines, or both. "Didn't you hear what mother said if we weren't back before dark, Jan? She'd boil our heads for supper!" Jan pointed to the mouth of a cave in the distance. Their mother was always making threats, but really she was as harmless as a turnip. Jacques withheld the fact that he'd previously seen the entrance to the cave in a dream. "Whatever happens," Jan said, "I'm glad you're my brother."

# I Was in America

in the 80s and 90s. People liked to stay alive forever by
swallowing big mouthfuls of porch light every evening. I had
a mini-Aztec pyramid dad built for me. The bees would go
up there and sacrifice themselves. The neighbors were bored
of living. Dad would conjure cardinals out of an oil drum.

"Please, call me Mom," he said, but mishearing him over the
sound of his chainsaw, I called him Moon.

It was Moon who played the guitar made out of cordwood
and wire.

It was Moon who called me last month, out of the blue.

## The Head in the Wall

The Head in the Wall sees things. The Head in the Wall doesn't know who put it there, but it lives out its days with few complaints. The Head is not a rebel. In fact, The Head hates rebels. The Head believes you play with the head you're dealt. When the family moved in, the first item of business was to tear down walls, in the name of the hysteria of open floor plans sweeping that rotten republic. So down the walls came and then the Head in the Wall was the Head in the Rubble, which was a little worse than before but not intolerable. Lacking digits with which to count, the Head whistled its blessings. Then this family, with great histrionics, scooped up the rubble and pushed it all out to sea on a raft. Then it was the Head in the Rubble Out to Sea on a Raft, the cold sloshing forever and crybaby stars. And the family? Well, you can't run from family, either.

# *Pipes*

Yesterday, Tony Paranoia pulled me aside and said he was thinking about taking up the uilleann pipes. I said "Well, T, I think uilleann pipes are sort of a life's project. Not just like picking up the ukulele and learning the chords to Rocky Raccoon."

He looked at me like I was nuts.

"Rocky Raccoon? It's from the White Album. Remember the White Album?"

But it was too late. He was already wandering the green fields of Sligo. His hands were ascending. His body was music. I rested my head on a Gideons bible and said, "How could you do this to me, T?"

# *What I Want From You*

I want you to write a letter explaining to me why you're not an asshole. I want you to tell me why the judge was wrong, why it was wrong of him to rule that you're an asshole and sentence you to fuck off. I want you to leave no stone unturned in your attempt at explaining why you are not, in fact, an actual hole that shit comes out of. I want you to convey to me in as many words as it takes why you qualify for affection from literally any living soul. I want you to go for a long walk and think about how to construct your thesis. I want this walk to go on for years if it has to. I want you to be explicit. I want that explicitness to come across in this letter in which you will stop at nothing to convince me, a concerned party, that you, an asshole in the eyes of the court, have been wrongly accused, convicted, and sentenced. I want you to say, in all sincerity, that if a doctor were to examine you, they would conclude that you are definitively not a body part which is an anus. I want you to know that I don't care which other body part this is, be it an arm, an appendix, or ears that hear what I am saying. I want you to introduce your argument with a little style, OK? I want you to quote Wordsworth or whatever. I want you to want the facts as bad as I want them. I want you to be invested in seeing this matter resolved. I want you to go into it with the assumption that after all is said and done you'll be inducted into the Never-Even-Was-An-Asshole-To-Begin-With club, and I'll be there, clapping and giving you two thumbs up. I want you to accept, right now, that this is going over no matter what. I want you to know I stay up nights listening to the static, waiting for you to wake up and get on with it.

# *Night Memo*

Stiff upper lip was never the issue. I'm talking about the
other one. Rain and the fire of my dreams. Country songs.
My old tired head. That was the issue. Animals born at the
zoo were the issue. Animals born in the wild. Japanese
beetles. Lanternflies. Kudzu was the issue. At night I'd press
my hand against it. But it was fake. Lost my hand. A million
and six bugs swarming at the concession stand window,
Hampshire County, West Virginia. I drank coffee and tried
to stage an intervention. Lost my other hand. Hotter on the
dark road home. I make a list of things to do before I die. I
make a list and lose it. I've never died. It's not an issue. Some
things put out a light so small you can't see it. That's not me.

## *Fight*

Yesterday, I went to my dream, the high school football game. Autumn burning cold and bright, but I didn't let it ruin my evening. The announcers sounded like underwater lawyers, but I didn't let it ruin my evening. No one could remember the fight song, but we sang loud. Then the kick went up, and it was good. Half of us got to live.

# *Vision*

Yesterday, I regressed to my 1 year old self. I needed to be changed, so I changed into someone who needs to be changed. I understood there was a sound which was what people called me, and sounds that meant do that or don't do that. I was afraid of food and animals. I had a vision of a twin. Then we found a perfectly good Jacques in the crawlspace.

## Stunt

Yesterday, Jacques regressed to his 1 year old self. His face was covered in brown baby gruel and he could barely string two words together. "Is this another stunt to get mom's attention?" I said. "Because she's been through enough." Then Alison walked in and said that it was her baby, as in my nephew, and I had been at the hospital when he was born, 12 months ago.

## *The Id Squad*

The Id Squad is here, rattling chains and wringing each other's necks. I am awake at the hour I normally am, which is this one.

From my second story window, I smell the booze steaming out of them. I hear them fucking right on the hot summer asphalt.

Their voices carry through the night, a quilt of whitewater and acceleration.

I want to yell shut-up, I'm trying to sleep.

But that would be a lie. And no one lies to the Id Squad.

## Plato's Man Cave

What of all these men, constructing and constructed by
the things they see and seem in their dreams? You couldn't
bring them back if you tried. Then there's the other matter
of the lost hikers. And the other other matter of the gangs
of toughs. OK, you say, what do you know about either?
Steady I say, here's what I know. The gangs of toughs never
talk about themselves because anyone could be listening and
the night is not safe. Lost hikers never stop talking, about
themselves or whatever really, they follow their echoing
voices echoing echoing until they arrive at lost. It's the people
with the least trouble to start with who are always out looking
for more. That's why I've never found any occupation more
suited to me than being a fake doctor. Down the line, I fear
we will discover many of our lost hikers will have done their
losing in the man caves of America. OK, you say, what do
you know about the man caves of America? Well, you were
hiking, for a long time, until you hiked into a dream. It is a
dream to me, but my man cave to you. That's what makes
this so difficult.

# Relief of My Symptoms

I.

I want to live where I don't have to. Black tea with the reaper under a sky pink as Pepto Bismol. I want to see the blood inside the snow and I want to know whether or not it matters if I touch it.

II.

You're row, row, rowing your boat, knowing, knowing, knowing. But here's the rub - you haven't even put your boat in the water. No need to work harder, or smarter. This is the Tao, gentle and dumb.

# Rather Than Admit to You My True Feelings

It's the story of the fortune teller who walked so far she died
It's the story of the thing in the hallway
It's the story of the pig made out of money
It's the story of the blind coconut the sun over Spain
It's the story of all the constellations you can eat
It's the story of a little lovemaking nearly inside the fireplace
It's the story of horses disappearing and reappearing
It's the story of summer bird autumn trees
It's the story of load bearing walls
It's the story of using the pan to flip the flapjack
It's the story of tears tears tears
It's the story of bad things happening to bad people
It's the story of the pop-punk commune and a surprisingly serious tone
It's the story of debts inevitable
It's the story of life on the mud planet
It's the story of the making of the resurrection of the growing boy
It's the story of why you moved to Tennessee to upset your mama
It's the story of knocking on doors mixing messages
It's the story of why you can never have a crispy skin like a turkey
It's the story of animal voices and how to stop hearing them
It's the story of the lineman lashed to a parking meter
It's the story of lightning striking the basement
It's the story of insubstantiality on tour with the flower brigade
It's the story of a playwright who once owned a mushroom
It's the story of a growing crust which has been promised your eyes
It's the story of the flow chart and what it will next time attempt to convey
It's the story of one held too closely too near the middle of their night
It's the story of a new girlfriend at every coffee shop
It's the story of the most puerile joke ever told a true barn burner

It's the story of outwitting yourself in the bathtub
It's the story of wild nights down at the wood shop
It's the story of what's this a pleasant aroma
It's the story of lord they bought it all all that howling acreage
It's the story of Give 'Em Enough Rope the oscillating tower fan
It's the story of pull apart bread or the brink of cinnamon
It's the story of a plastic antlersphere
It's the story of drinking six hours a mere misdemeanor
It's the story of why we drift and the temperature of pain
It's the story of nice turn signal
It's the story of closed today since that cloud is a raccoon
It's the story of the gourmand and the sleuth God helps us
It's the story of finding astonishingly even worse hands in my pockets
It's the story of shadows or how we all block the sun

## Mr. Cloudblood

Sitting on my porch in the early evening,
I get a feeling like the blood

in my veins is clouds
in the sky, and I must race
across town to save a life.

Then the sun goes
down and I go
inside and the feeling is gone.

## *Lost in the Waves*

Gather, children, around
this fire. Tonight,
there is no story to be told
but our own.

Before we walked on land,
humans were just ghosts, lost
in the waves. I am tired
already, from looking at you
and breathing the smoke.

Today we are the same, maybe
more wide ranging. From dust bowl
to milk bowl. The great scholars
all nod in agreement.

Children do you ever say anything?
I am loitering here, with the worst
ideas of our moment.

As a matter of fact, I knew each of you
when you were worse than ideas.
That is to say, I knew your parents.
Oh the wonders
of their interior architecture.
And so my youth was spent.

Whatever I share with you, I beg

you to share with others.
It's a way to live on. You won't
learn anything as great in your school books.

Not that I'm against books.
I wrote a book. It's called "How to
Breathe Smoke and Retire
on a Mealworm's Pension". It's out of print.
See the stars? They're retired too,
but on not so fixed an income.
One day you will make little
parables out of them, that not even
you yourselves will heed.

What happens when we don't
heed our own advice? It's a version
of "Lost in the Waves", written
by the ghostly mealworm himself.

Here we are, my handsome hatchlings, at the end
of human wisdom. And no money
for a return ticket. Unless . . .
you didn't bring any money, did you?

Forgive me. I've breathed
so much smoke and looked
so long at your faces,
I feel like hell's first prisoner.

**II**

# City of Smoke

This family lived in a city made out of smoke. The downspouts, fire escapes, fruit vendors, little dogs, big dogs, and the family themselves, all smoke. The city of smoke was located on the island of smoke, in the country of smoke, on the planet of smoke.

The only things that weren't made out of smoke were their hopes and dreams. To be a world class typist, to have off on Sundays. Those things were real, like the iron bars of another planet they'd read about in books made of smoke.

# Up

I think the river will rise tonight and like a country boy go for a stroll. And if angels in fiery robes fall from the sky, I've seen them before. Fernando Pessoa once wrote "all it would take to make a catalogue of monsters is to photograph in words the things the night brings to drowsy souls unable to sleep." But when the black cat brings me a bird, I kiss both wings, I kiss both paws.

## *Forest*

Yesterday, I was telling a fat bunch of lies to all my jackass friends about how they're not a bunch of jackasses and that our friendship is real, like the trees in the forest are real or death by lethal injection is real. But I didn't include the similes, because then those jackasses would've known I was telling them a fat bunch of lies.

# War

Yesterday, I was up in the attic with Jacques shooting a lot of guns. He has so many - handguns, rifles, machine guns. He's even got one from the revolutionary war. "Who'd you have to blow to get that one?" I asked him. "If I told you," he said, "you'd probably wish you weren't my brother anymore." The silhouette of Benjamin Franklin appeared on the wall. I let it go.

# *Passing Time With You*

Passing time with you is grand oh it's a monkey's game
Passing time with you at the discount furniture outlet
Passing time with you while we both hold our breath
Passing time with you must be what I've been waiting for
I waited while it hid in the ragged sleeves of the Earth
Passing time with you and our families
Our families and their arguments and the spittle hitting the air
Passing time with you feels medieval minus the straw floors and dead bodies
Well, some dead bodies
Passing time with you I feel like a man who's been taught how to fish but not
how to swim oh it's a sailor's game all this passing time with you
You help me to remember to floss twice
Passing time with you like there's no tomorrow
Passing time with you like there's no yesterday
Passing time with you like today is the last can of beans in the cupboard
Passing time with you I lied and told you I was an Aries and you said
that explains a lot
Passing time with you always adding to my apologia
Passing time with you in the great cities of Appalachia
Passing time with you head is heavy heart's sprung a big break
Passing time with you at the George Jones museum
Yes there is such a thing as the George Jones museum
Passing time with you is nothing compared to passing time with you
Tell those oily birds to get the fuck off of my porch can't get anything done
with those oily birds all over my porch
Passing time with you my head's a balloon let it go

A friend is a forest there is darkness there are mushrooms

When we are together time kills itself

# *What to Do With Your Wealth*

I woke up this morning and discovered that I was wealthy beyond my wildest dreams. But how? I quickly determined this wasn't important, in the sense that nothing is important, so all the better to get there fast.

Secondly I determined I was determined to spend my wealth on useless things, because the fastest way to change a useless thing into a useful thing is to buy it.

But before I could do any of that, I needed to get the shovel out of the garage and leave it in the rain, because a shovel looks so good sitting out in the rain. It's the rain that gives it a mind of its own.

Then I needed to check my bird feeders - no birds anywhere as I'd forgotten to fill the feeders for months. This absence also seemed to have its own mind, one made sharper by the rain falling harder by the minute.

Feeling caught up, I checked my weather app. "Rivers to flood stage in one hour," it said. "Grab belongings and flee like fleas."

Well this is just fine, I thought, as towns upstate which were not about to be underwater had some of the finest goods, goods much finer than any I've ever been able to find around here.

But first I needed to find my keys, so I could place them in a hole in the ground. It's the time spent underground that gives keys their magic power to start a vehicle or open doors. While I was waiting, I packed my bags. Toothbrush, check. Socks, check. Smaller bags to be inserted into larger bags - numbering in the thousands, as God intended.

But before I could finish packing, I remembered I needed to burn my house down. Burning one's house down with all of one's wealth and one's entire body inside it is the only way to keep warm during a flood.

# The Governor and the Pig

The governor had been busy all day trying to wrangle a pig. The pig had seven names. The pig said "all you have to do is speak my seven names one time each, and you can do whatever you want with me, pick me up and take me wherever."

The governor was not about to speak even one of the pig's names, let alone seven. The governor wanted to wrangle the pig on his own terms.

As night fell on the state wrangling grounds, it became clear neither were going to give in.

"Why does this always happen to me?" thought the governor, the pig having the same thought. No one was around. Not even the moon was watching.

Eventually, fatigue overtook them and they fell into a dangerous sleep out in the elements. An aide found them the next morning, being picked at by birds of carrion.

Seven birds, and not a single name between them.

## *Activity*

Yesterday, we divided up the pigs. Some were sent underground. Others were sent up into the sky on a plane then dropped on the ground. The pigs that went underground we never saw again. The pigs dropped out of the plane we see everywhere now. This is an activity we did as a family.

## Back to the Land

Ants run up the leg of a scarecrow. The scarecrow says "Oh, that tickles!"

"Our business with you is very serious," the ants say. "It should not tickle."

"I'm on fire, please have mercy on me," the scarecrow says.

The ants don't say "that's more like it," because, like what?

It's hard work, a life up against the land.

# *Alison*

*I know this world is killing you*
-Elvis Costello

I was leading a group of kids into a wood between
subdivisions, telling them "our ancestors were scared, too."

In our town, every day opens with a musical number.

In our town, the grocery baggers dream of being cashiers,
and the cashiers dream of being groceries.

These kids were a real bunch of know-nothings. Poseurs in
dog shorts. They didn't even have cigarettes.

While lecturing them about the dangers of moss, one kid ran
off to drum on the bones of a boar.

I asked if any of them had ever listened to Iron Maiden.

Then I looked around and didn't see Alison. "Alison? Where's
Alison?" I asked.

None of them could remember an Alison.

# *Prank*

Yesterday, I was pretty sure someone was playing a prank on me. I got in my car and the framed photo of my brother and sister and my mom and dad and the dogs in front of the persimmon tree at my grandparents' house which I normally keep under the bed was sitting on the passenger seat. "This isn't funny!" I howled, thinking about how tears actually start in your mouth and then work their way up to the eyes. I started crying so hard, it was like being at the automatic carwash.

# *Tour of Benevolence*

I started out my tour of benevolence at the fire hall.

I was shaking hands with firefighters for what felt like days, doing that thing where I wrap two of my hands around one of theirs. "Seriously, great work, I mean it. You guys really do it all."

I made my way to the children's home, where each child received a kiss on the forehead and a single rose. They all had faces like wild lettuce, instantly forgettable faces.

Then I went to visit Jacques at his job at the diner, but the diner was on fire. Jacques was standing out front in his little paper hat, looking "zen". I regretted paying the firefighters so many compliments. I started to compose a letter to the fire marshal in my mind - "I have never seen such irresponsibility . . ."

My tour of benevolence was wrapping up. Only one more stop: dear Anthony in the hospital. I put a paper bag over my head, slipped into his room, and said "Here I am, your very own death. See? Not so bad, eh? Not so bad." He screamed and took a swing at me, causing the I.V. to pop out of his arm in the manner of a wild fire hose.

## *Centaurs*

The judge ruled that I was an asshole and my sentence was to fuck off. The bailiff escorted me out the door, where my fucking off was to begin. A light rain did not begin to fall. I rubbed my lucky salamander tail, an old mummy thing.

All in all, I was found guilty on 93 counts of being an asshole. 93 is a nice sounding number, I thought. Maybe I could work some numerology into this and get a fresh perspective on things.

9 plus 3 is 12. I have 2 lucky salamander tails - one for at home and one for on the go. 12 divided by 2 is 6. Turn the 6 on its side and smoke it like a lighthouse keeper's pipe. Use the light from the lighthouse to navigate to the judge's house. Estimate this taking 2 hours, 1 hour for every centaur meeting me at the judge's house.

Tell the centaurs when we get there it's time to step on him.

4 legs per centaur equals 8 legs crushing 1 judge. Seems like overkill. Overkill is a nice sounding word. I'm allowed to say it as much as I like.

## *Achievement*

Yesterday, I overheard Jacques talking about "shitting a brick." I was amazed - had he really, and how? Or why? I searched all over for this brick, assuming it would be easy to find because of the smell. While searching the yard, I saw my brother up in the attic, watching me, with a look on his face that said I would forever be grasping at the achievements of others. I shot a look back at him that said "you're a fucking liar."

## Fan Club

I wake up to the sound of cheering outside my window. I pull back the curtains, and see a crowd of people standing in the yard, waving signs that say WAY TO GO and YOU DID IT.

I open the window and ask, "what's all this for?"

"Way to go!" someone yells. "You did it!" yells another.

"Yes, but what did I do?" I ask again.

They all take one step forward.

# III

# The Wildcat

I love golf, and the courses it's played on. I love the way the moon shines down on the trees at night, when I go out there to do my dirty business. Instantly, I morph into a wildcat who has to shit whenever I even glance at a sand trap. My father was a man who ate two loaves of bread a day and played pedal steel in a country band. He also loved to golf. That man lived for three things only - loaves, links, and his lover, steel. Sometimes, I think about him and the things he loved. And then I think about how I did love him, even though he didn't seem to love me, or if he did, he was good at hiding it. Look, we were talking about golf. I already told you about the moon glinting off the fucking trees at night, and taking uninhibited feral shits in the sand traps. But equally as important to me are the nights spent at the bottom of the ponds, where the bones of golfers past form a boardwalk to hell. On his dying bed, my father told me he dreamt of God calling the Devil to reserve him a spot in the fiery place. Now every night I dream his dream. Only in my version I'm holding a tarantula, feeding it slices of peaches. There's a gun on the wall. Just for decoration.

# The Art of Hunting

This guy got his son up before dawn to teach him the art of hunting. The idea is to go out into the woods and find a big juicy animal to penetrate with bullets. This guy really wanted his son to shoot one. It would make him so proud. A young warrior in bloom. How great if he shot one right in between the eyes, or even in the eye! No cell phones, no distractions, just two men following a blood trail. They'd drag it a mile out of the woods which would make them good and tired. It is American to be good and tired. It is also very American to get the animal's juices all over you. This guy couldn't wait to show him how to skin it. "Here's the liver," he would say, and the early afternoon sun golden as the heart of God, golden as the hearts of the ghosts of pioneers still watching over those woods, hallelujah. "Look, a family of turkeys," this guy would whisper, and not shoot them. It is American to know when not to shoot.

# The Curse

*Turn on the tea and let it brew*
-Michael Hurley

Anthony was a large man who would often shake with laughter, like a washing machine that loved you. One day, after telling him the joke about the two dogs caught in a lightning storm, he shook so hard his heart stopped. I was drinking a cup of tea. I remember the tea burned my tongue quite badly, and I was upset - with myself, but mostly with the tea. I cursed the day we ever crossed paths, the tea and I. At his funeral, I got up and told the joke. Everyone's tears of sadness got mixed up with their tears of laughter. Blood and milk. It's funny because it's true. The dogs always come back, but they're never the same.

## *Loop*

Yesterday, I found myself lost in a feedback loop about coolness, the personality trait. The loop would go like this - you are not lost. You are just alone. But then, if you are alone, why are you alone? Because you are lost and it is not cool to be lost. But you are not lost, you are just alone. But then, if you are alone, why are you alone? Because you are lost and it is not cool to be lost. But you are not lost . . .

## The Light of Day

I'm pretty tough, but not as tough as my sister. One time, I saw her take four guys at once - to their respective therapist appointments. "The book of our lives is a special book because it's the only one that gets heavier as you tear out the pages," she said to me. We had a little orchard we liked to run through in our minds. "Full solar eclipses always make my nose bleed," is something else she said, then demonstrated. Back then, I wasn't tough enough to take anyone at their word.

## *Storm*

Yesterday, I became suddenly aware of the possibility of writing about my own, real, life and letting other people read it. So I sat down, with my greatest pencil and emptiest notebook, and began to commit many true things about my life to paper, which I then typed up on a computer. Then I printed the pages, stuffed them in envelopes, addressed them to family and friends, put stamps on them, and walked outside and dropped them down a storm drain. Then I put my face up against the drain and remembered astrology. I waited with my face in this drain for hours, certain that the secrets of astrology would soon be revealed to me. When it got dark, I went home.

# Self Portrait at 35

Bad in the sense of very cool. Fond of the joke about the farmer who won an award. Lost some weight, lost some tooth. Still wrapping my bones in skin and my skin in clothes as per tradition. Occasionally up high looking down, occasionally down low not looking. Passable oxygenation throughout most tissues. A little bigger than my brother and a little smaller than my other brother. Some thoughts arctic, others dipped in fire. Inventor of the leaning post - still my greatest achievement. Have quelled bigger part of the urge to die. Not necessarily looking at what you're pointing at. More likely just looking at your finger. Enchanted by fingers because they are very traditional. In present tense - am living. In past - I did that to live. Open 7 days a week.

*For David Berman*

## *Palida Luña*

Whenever I leave on a trip, I sit down with my ghost and say "I'm going out, you stay here." By this time tomorrow, I intend to be standing on a tall rock, holding hands with Lydia Mendoza. Until then, I'll settle for this dream behind the wheel, where I'm walking to the top of the burial mound in South Charleston, West Virginia, across from Suzi's Drive In, under a moon close and calm as a nurse's hand. The last thing my grandfather ever said to me was "you're gonna make me cry," and I did.

# *The Fall of Batman*

Yesterday, Batman's wings malfunctioned and he fell off
a building onto his back. That was all for Batman. The
Joker, The Riddler, Two-Face, and Catwoman showed up to
pallbear him across the city. The same black rain that's always
fallen on Gotham was falling.

Alfred decided he would put on the suit and resume the fight.
Who said his best days were behind him?

But then came Gotham's most heinous villain yet: The
Enabler.

# We Have People for That

Sometimes, when you go to the movies, at the end, people stand up and clap. I guess it's because they're proud of each other. Don't be afraid to join them. You look beautiful in there, after all, like a cowboy by the fire, about to break into song. Sometimes in the movie there's a drag race, or an old man walking alone in the desert. Sometimes two images are shown superimposed on each other. The effect is *dizzying*, as they say in the biz. It's important to take stock of the sensations a movie allows you to feel without having to get up out of your seat or even move at all. The *delights*, they're called, another industry term. At the end of everything, though, remember, it's all an illusion, just some obscenely rich people having a little bit of fun at their own expense, and yours, too. Do not grow a beard, dress in rags, and wander like the face of starvation himself into the city's blue welter. We have people for that.

## Soup

Yesterday, I was feeling sick, so I took what I had lying around and made some soup. God it was boring, standing there, making soup, and then afterward, knowing I had to eat it. I felt so sick and so bored. I'm glad that day is over.

## By Our Infinite Powers Combined

The weather is a wall
The forest is a virtual reality cage
The endangered species list is a manifest
The diamond is an afterthought
The recessive gene is a double tongued forefinger
The man sleeping on the street is a door
The burn unit is a seminar
The gut-shot outlaw is a fine tooth comb
The beady-eyed double is a rodent with rights
The harsh and unforgiving landscape is an archtop guitar
The cluster of stinkbugs is a brooch
The circus organ jig is a rebuttal to what made the land and sea
The wart encrusted blister is a blessing etched in marble
The aerosol can is a dull talon
The dismal hollow is a perfect circle
The delayed flight is a note sung in an empty room
The figure of speech is a ghoul drinking from a hose
The doted upon son is a ghost's dragging chain
The season of floods and ice is an editor
The train carrying souls to hell is a tentative yes
The halftime show is a powdered wig on the wind
The retinal scanner is a dab of this and that
The decommissioned shopping mall is a cub traveling by moonlight
The glimmer of remorse is a spider more bitsy than itsy
The warrior burning his clothes is a result near you
The rolling thunder is an entire nation gone out for a smoke

The vanishing point is a chisel held to God's throat
The common denominator is a demonic commentator
The sip is a gulp
The clam is a clone
The rope is a rush
The need to be touched is a figure thin as Nosferatu
The family photo album is a stunning concept
The cult of lemmings is a laughing quartet
The first grade classroom is a digital monastery
The groveling groveler is a grown man or me
The last person left on Earth is a willing participant

# A Visit to the Grand Canyon

People like to talk
about the grand scheme
of things, and things
in and of themselves,
and things that have
been on their mind lately.

They like to talk about
rhythm being a thing
that one either has or doesn't,
and they like to talk,
ad infinitum, about
the things of this world.
They will also mention

this thing that's growing
inside them, which gives them
pause. And inside that pause,
the water is rising, and inside
that water, a thing of beauty
which is, of course,
drowning. They will stop

you in the middle of what
you're saying and say
"that's just the thing,"
and you are alone
in these moments, because

where are they going with that?
You thought all things
were in your sight.
And you say, no, I don't mind

being alone, but typically,
I prefer to go down
to the water to be alone,
not to be completely and
desperately alone in the company of
another person. That's the thing
that bugs you - all this talk

about talent and temperament
and hey cheer up, things
will turn around sooner
or later, something often said
and rarely believed. Consolation
erodes belief, like surf
into cliffs, and I think

that's in the bible, actually,
right after the thing about how
God doesn't take things
personally, doesn't need
or want anything from you,
it is you that is the needing
and wanting thing, and God's
interest rates are fixed, anyway,
so you can thank him for that.

I have too many things
in my house, too many things
on my to-do list, too many
things standing in my way,
too many symbols, signs,
and wonders, the light
of the sun, the cool
of the clouds - who is chasing who,
and these things they cling,
like monkeys to branches,
or people to life, all its scrapes
and burns and blood-
baths, meteor showers.

And they say, who says,
no one says a love of life is a love
of blood as it falls from the sky
or erupts from the Earth,

except for me, I am the one
saying it, to you, right now,
it is the thing I am
saying and have been saying
this entire time.

# *Strong Return*

Perspectives on antics,
grapes, and streams
Thanks, Ma

If your thoughts are about the last American
I will fly away
Much prefer to forge in dust and Duck, Daffy

and Taz

They are rising
out of the river someone
wants them home

I wish the syllables would take their katydids
elsewhere as it is

If you see a moth ever ride
a katydid into the moon rise

If not, call me
You can
always call me

Acknowledgments

"Comfort, Redefined" first appeared in Pithead Chapel

"Ancient Grains" "Over Creeks and Pastures" and "The Head in the Wall" first appeared in Hello America Stereo Cassette

"Palida Luña" first appeared in Hobart

"The Art of Hunting" first appeared in The Travelin' Appalachians Revue

"By Our Infinite Powers Combined" and "We Have People for That" first appeared in Rabid Oak

"Fight" "Up" "The Curse" and "The Light of Day" first appeared in the chapbook *Holy Gravel,* published by Ghost Palace Press.

Thanks to Mom, Dad, Drew, Ty, Seth Pitt, Shaemus Spencer, and Carina Cass.